D1244535

FINDING YOUR IDENTITY

By Kate Morrow

CONTENT CONSULTANT

Jenny Oliphant, EdD, MPH
Community Outreach Coordinator and Research Associate
Healthy Youth Development-Prevention Research Center
University of Minnesota
School of Medicine, Division of General Pediatrics and Adolescent Health

Essential Library

An Imprint of Abdo Publishing | abdobooks.com

abdobooks.com

Printed in the United States of America, North Mankato, Minnesota.
082020
012021

THIS BOOK CONTAINS
RECYCLED MATERIALS

Cover Photo: Gustavo Araújo/Pexels
Interior Photos: iStockphoto, 8, 40, 61, 70–71, 78, 84, 90; Jacob Lund/iStockphoto, 10–11, 46; Son Hoang Tran/Shutterstock Images, 12–13; SDI Productions/iStockphoto, 16–17; Zuraisham Salleh/iStockphoto, 20; Kristian Sekulic/iStockphoto, 22–23; Monkey Business Images/iStockphoto, 24, 68; Shutterstock Images, 28–29, 34, 49, 98–99; Atstock Productions/Shutterstock Images, 30; Martine Doucet/iStockphoto, 36–37; Michael Jung/Shutterstock Images, 42–43; Deepak Sethi/iStockphoto, 50; Jasmin Zurijeta/Shutterstock Images, 53; M Studio Images/iStockphoto, 54; Praetorian Photo/iStockphoto, 58; Lincoln Beddoe/Shutterstock Images, 62–63; Media Photos/iStockphoto, 74; Tarik Kizilkaya/iStockphoto, 81; Fotostorm/iStockphoto, 87; Wave Break Media/iStockphoto, 93; Wave Break Media/Shutterstock Images, 95

Editor: Megan Ellis
Series Designer: Nikki Nordby

Library of Congress Control Number: 2019954375
Publisher's Cataloging-in-Publication Data

Names: Morrow, Kate, author.
Title: Finding your identity / by Kate Morrow
Description: Minneapolis, Minnesota : Abdo Publishing, 2021 | Series: Strong, healthy girls | Includes online resources and index.
Identifiers: ISBN 9781532192173 (lib. bdg.) | ISBN 9781098210076 (ebook)
Subjects: LCSH: Identity (Psychology)--Juvenile literature. | Self in adolescence--Juvenile literature. | Identity, Ethnic--Juvenile literature. | Identity (Religion)--Juvenile literature. | Gender identity--Juvenile literature.
Classification: DDC 155.533--dc23

CONTENTS

DR. JENNY

Jenny Oliphant believes all young people deserve to thrive, not just survive. Her work focuses on making sure parents, professionals, and young people themselves have the information, skills, and tools to make that happen. She's an expert in adolescent sexual health, youth development, health education, and sports education.

Dr. Jenny holds a master's of public health in community health education from the University of Minnesota and a doctorate from the University of Saint Thomas in educational leadership. She speaks locally and nationally about youth development, peer education, and pregnancy prevention. Her background includes experiences as a health educator and adjunct instructor in health for community health educators, health teachers, and epidemiologists in training.

Dr. Jenny is the community outreach coordinator and research associate for the Healthy Youth Development-Prevention Research Center at the University of Minnesota in the School of Medicine, Division of General Pediatrics and Adolescent Health. There, she helps families and health providers design and implement youth-friendly health programming supported by current research. At Walden University, as a contributing faculty member, she teaches students the art and science of becoming community-engaged public health professionals working for social change.

Dr. Jenny teaches future pediatricians and nurses how to interview teens about their sexual health. She recently wrapped up a five-year study in which she worked with middle schools to develop teaching plans to improve students' social and emotional health. Her newest research is focused on helping clinics better engage with adolescent patients. She's also working on training dentists and hygienists to recommend the human papillomavirus vaccine to parents and young people.

Dr. Jenny has worked as a consultant for a series of books written for teens and focused on topics in adolescent health. She's also served as a federal accuracy reviewer for numerous curricula used in programming funded by the US government's Office of Adolescent Health.

She lives in Minneapolis, Minnesota, with her teen children, her husband, and her bulldog, Sid. In the future, she dreams of living and working in Berlin, Germany, and continues to practice her German, in hopes of making her dream come true.

TAKE IT
FROM ME

Your identity is made up of pieces of yourself, including your likes and dislikes, your beliefs, and your gender identity and expression. You use these pieces to show other people who you are. I didn't sit down and think about my identity very often while I was in school. Mostly I was concerned with whether the school cafeteria was serving chicken nuggets for lunch, how to get my science homework done, and which fantasy book I could next check out from the library. I cared about winning an argument with my friend about whether superheroes were only for boys or whether girls could like them too. And in speech class, I worried about defending what I believed without crying, because talking about things close to my heart made me teary-eyed.

However, even though I didn't classify any of this as active work toward figuring out my identity, I was well on my way to understanding who I was. Even though I wasn't actively thinking about making changes, I was putting my potential self into action every day.

Learning to know yourself is one of the healthiest things a girl can do. Being confident in your likes and dislikes, your beliefs, your strengths and weaknesses—all of this helps you figure out how you fit into the world around you. This might seem like a scary thing. It was to me. I was nervous that I had to have such a strong understanding of myself. How do you study for a test like that? But one important thing I've realized is that your identity isn't something you have to decide in a certain time frame. It's not made up of a checklist of beliefs and ideas. It isn't even something you're stuck with for your entire life. To me, finding your identity is a process. You assemble it in bits and pieces. It's built on a foundation of everything you've seen and experienced, read and absorbed. And an identity is always evolving. You're not stuck with who you might have been once. You always have the option to change who you want to be. There is no wrong way to start assembling the parts of what makes you *you*.

YOUR FRIEND,
KATE

CHAPTER ONE

FINDING YOUR INTERESTS

Have you ever pretended to like something because your friends did and you didn't want to feel left out of the group? Many people want to feel like they belong. Stories about people belonging and not belonging show up in movies, books, and TV shows. Often, teenagers in these stories have a hard time fitting in until they meet a group of people who really understand them.

Wanting to fit in is normal. We all want people in our lives who will accept and appreciate us. When you're young, one of the easiest ways to create those bonds is to share the same interests as those closest to you. But as you get older, you may find that you develop interests outside of your friend group. You may prefer action movies while your friends like musicals. Maybe you discover that you love hockey, but all of your friends prefer football. Or maybe you get super involved with the yearbook club while your friends choose to do marching band.

> Discovering your own interests is part of understanding your identity.

Discovering your own interests is part of understanding your identity. But fitting in can feel more difficult as your interests diverge, or split. You may be tempted to keep your newfound interests secret from your friends so they don't move on without you. You also might make new friends who are interested in your new favorite sports or clubs. In those cases, it might seem like you no longer fit with your old friend group in the way you used to.

KAYLEE'S STORY

Kaylee and her friends, Cory and Jazz, had always loved listening to the Top 40 station on their radio app. Ever since they started being friends in fourth grade, everything they did was to the soundtrack of American pop music, including sleepovers, car rides to the movie theater, and dance class after school. Once a month, they even sat down and picked their new favorite song

from the app and put the lyrics on all their social media profiles. It was their ritual—something they always did together.

But a few months back, Kaylee became super interested in South Korean pop music, or K-pop. She'd stumbled across a few videos of different K-pop groups online. She loved the cheerful beats of their music, their amazing music videos, and the way so many of the musicians were also incredible dancers.

Kaylee still listened to the Top 40 station when she was with her friends, but on her own, she listened almost exclusively to K-pop. She started researching the bands, watching their concert footage online, and following their social media accounts. Sometimes, she caught herself about to blurt out an interesting fact about one of her favorite K-pop groups in front of her friends. But every time, Kaylee decided not to speak up. She was embarrassed to be so interested in something her friends knew nothing about. She thought they might judge her for having this new taste in music. She tried to play one song for them once, but Cory and Jazz didn't seem to like it very much.

TALK ABOUT IT

= Why do you think Kaylee felt like she needed to keep her new love of K-pop secret from her friends?

= Do you think Kaylee's friends should have handled it differently when Kaylee played a K-pop song for them? What could they have done instead?

= Have you ever developed a new interest and felt like you had to hide it? How did it feel?

Kaylee kept her love of K-pop a secret. But having no one to talk to about something she was so passionate about made her feel lonely. One day in her economics class, Kaylee caught sight of a sticker on another girl's notebook. It was a sticker for one of Kaylee's favorite K-pop groups. The girl saw Kaylee staring and asked if she'd heard of the group. Kaylee said that she had.

"I love their music!" Kaylee said.

"Me too," the girl, Amber, agreed. "What did you think of their latest song?"

"It was incredible!" Kaylee spoke quickly, like the words she'd been bottling up were suddenly rushing out all at once. "Did you see the music video?"

Amber launched into a step-by-step analysis of the music video, and she and Kaylee spent the rest of work time in class whispering about their favorite groups.

***

Soon, Amber and Kaylee started coming to class early each day so they could talk about K-pop before the bell rang. Then Kaylee started eating lunch with Amber instead of her other friends. She'd go to Amber's house after school, and they'd listen to their favorite groups. Kaylee decorated her notebooks with stickers of her own, and she and

TALK ABOUT IT

= Why do you think Kaylee's friends were upset with her?

= Why do you think Kaylee was so excited to meet Amber? How could she have handled the situation differently?

Amber talked about forming a K-pop club at school.

It made Kaylee happy to find someone who really understood her musical interests. She wanted to share her excitement with her other friends now that she felt like she wasn't the only one in the world who liked K-pop. But the next time Kaylee chose to eat lunch with Cory and Jazz, they were both upset with her.

"You've been ignoring us for weeks," said Jazz.

"And every time we did get ahold of you, you said you already had plans," added Cory. "Do you not want to be friends anymore?"

TALK ABOUT IT

= **Have you ever had friends drift away because they fell in with a new group or interest? How did it feel?**

= **Have you ever drifted away from a friend group? How did the group react?**

= **Do you think Kaylee and her friends resolved the situation well? Would you have done anything differently?**

"Do you not want to be friends anymore?"

Kaylee was shocked. The idea of not wanting to be friends with Jazz and Cory had never even occurred to her. She'd just gotten so wrapped up in sharing her love of K-pop with Amber.

Kaylee explained what she'd been doing with Amber. She talked about hiding her love of K-pop from Jazz and Cory.

15

"I'm sorry," she said. "I didn't mean to avoid you or stop hanging out with you! I just wanted to talk to someone about K-pop."

"Just because we don't like K-pop doesn't mean we don't like you," Jazz pointed out.

"We don't want you to stop listening to music you like," Cory added. "But we'd still like to see you too."

Kaylee apologized again. From then on, she worked harder at splitting her time between Amber and her other friends. Jazz and Cory made a point of showing interest in Kaylee's K-pop music even if it still wasn't their favorite. They asked how Kaylee and Amber's club was going and looked at pictures of the concert Kaylee and Amber went to see. In return, Kaylee made a point of going to Cory's choir concerts and cheering on the soccer team Jazz had joined.

"Just because we don't like K-pop doesn't mean we don't like you."

EXPERT

Kaylee hid her love of K-pop from her friends because she knew they didn't share her interest in it. She felt like being different from them meant that she no longer fit in. Once she met Amber, Kaylee got swept up in a new sense of belonging, but she hurt the friends she'd already had by excluding them from her life.

Having different interests than your friends doesn't mean you no longer belong with them. Similar to the way a puzzle is made up of differently shaped pieces, fitting in doesn't mean being identical. Pursuing what you're passionate about shows that you're able to establish an identity that's different from your friends. And respecting the varying interests of others shows that you can honor and appreciate identities outside of your own. Kaylee felt uncertain about where she fit in after developing an interest different from that of her friends. But she felt like she belonged even more once she found a friend who shared her interest, as well as a way to still hang out with the ones who didn't.

Kaylee didn't have to stop being friends with Cory and Jazz just because she had a common interest with Amber. Instead, Kaylee and her friends found a way to support their differing interests and still fit together.

GET **HEALTHY**

- Keep your friends up to date on your interests and activities. They can't know your life if you don't share it.

- Don't be afraid to expand your social circle, but be sure you're making time for all of your important people. Feeling left out is never fun.

- Explore what interests you, even if it's something your friends aren't equally interested in. Having a unique identity means pursuing what you're passionate about!

- Respect interests and activities that your friends have, even if you don't share them. Fitting in means supporting each other, even if your friends' interests aren't your favorite thing.

THE LAST WORD FROM **KATE**

What interests you will shift and change as you grow and explore. That doesn't necessarily mean that your friend group has to change or that you no longer belong. It might mean that you fit in a different way. Maybe new interests will mean adding new friends or activities. And even if changing interests means you lose touch with the friends you had before, that doesn't mean you did anything wrong, as long as you part ways with love and respect.

It's OK to explore new ideas and activities. Whether it's K-pop or Top 40, soap operas or anime, automotive care or interior decorating, the world of interests is so large and rich with opportunity. What you're passionate about can help define who you are and maybe even lead to a future career. Figuring out those passions early on can lay the groundwork for who you want to be later.

CHAPTER TWO

IDENTIFYING YOUR STRENGTHS

D o you have a friend who seems to magically navigate their way around a city without getting lost? Or a family member who can total up the grocery bill before even getting to the checkout register? Do you know someone who seems comfortable with any group of people, even if they've just met?

We all have different strengths. Some of them are learned, and others we're born with. Maybe you have an ear for different languages. Maybe you have enough determination to push forward no matter what else might be going on around you. Or maybe you have a super sharp focus that allows you to target a goal and achieve it quickly.

It's important to know your strengths, whatever they may be. By understanding your strengths, you can shape your identity around what you can best bring to the world. You can tackle different situations and assignments with what you consider your greatest assets. When working with others, you can better match your strengths with theirs. Knowing your strengths can also help you advocate for yourself. If you're aware of your strengths, you can use them to do better at school, work, home, or even in your extracurricular activities.

Knowing your strengths can also help you advocate for yourself.

But how do you identify your strengths? And once you know them, how do you use them to help yourself be successful? Fatima struggled in some of her classes before she learned to use her strengths to help her succeed. This knowledge helped her tackle a tricky school situation.

FATIMA'S STORY

Fatima's English class was giving her the worst headache. Not because of the reading. Fatima loved to read, and the books her teacher had chosen this year were actually pretty interesting.

But every time they read a book, Mrs. Huang assigned a group project. The students were expected to explore the book's major themes using notes they took during class and then present on the themes as a group. The presentation part wasn't the problem. Fatima loved speaking in front of people. She could

easily talk for the entire presentation, but her group wanted to split the spoken presentation evenly to give everyone a chance to talk—even Tanner, who hated public speaking.

Fatima had a hard time with her note-taking. The group decided to split this work evenly too. But Fatima struggled with her notes. Mrs. Huang recommended that they take notes by picking out the most important parts of her lectures or of the books themselves. However, Fatima could never tell the difference between what was important and what was just supporting detail. She always ended up writing down everything she read or listened to in class, hoping that the important information would still be there. Unfortunately, this made her notes crowded and messy, especially when Mrs. Huang went through the slides too quickly. They were never useful when it came time to work on the project. Fatima felt terrible for being unable to help her group.

***

After finishing their most recent project, Fatima was shocked to see that she and Tanner had both received a lower grade than their groupmates.

"I can tell you have so much to contribute," Mrs. Huang explained when Fatima met with

TALK ABOUT IT

= Have you ever struggled with something that someone else found easy? How did it make you feel?

= Why do you think Fatima might be struggling?

her after class to understand her lower grade. "But every time your group submits their notes, I can tell that yours weren't as helpful in the research process. And because you only talk for a few minutes of the presentation, I can't know for sure that you really understand the material."

Fatima twisted her hands together in distress. "I'm just not as good at taking notes as the other people in my group. It's confusing for me."

"I can help you work on that in class," Mrs. Huang promised. "But until then, think about how you can best show what you know. If you can't score highly with your research notes, think about where you can make up those points."

"I'm just not as good at taking notes as the other people in my group."

***

As they started a new book for class, Fatima thought about what Mrs. Huang had said. As she promised, Mrs. Huang gave Fatima some tips and strategies for improving her note-taking. But Fatima could tell that her notes still wouldn't be helpful enough when the time came to explore the book's themes.

Fatima took out the group project rubric that Mrs. Huang had given the students at the beginning of the year. The rubric was made up of different categories that Mrs. Huang used to grade the group, both as a whole and as individual students. Fatima kept losing points in the Understanding of Material category due to her research notes. However, the notes weren't the only part of the category. Another bullet point in the category referred to being able to explain the material verbally.

Fatima had an idea. She caught up with Tanner in the hallway after class.

"Hey!" she said. "On our last group project, you got a lower grade too. Right?"

Tanner flushed and shuffled his feet. "Yeah. Because I'm no good at public speaking. I can't ever put what I think into words, and I end up sounding like I don't know what I'm talking about."

"But your notes are awesome," Fatima pointed out.

"I like taking notes," Tanner agreed. "But then I lose points on the speaking because it sounds like I don't understand."

"I'm no good at public speaking. I can't ever put what I think into words, and I end up sounding like I don't know what I'm talking about."

TALK ABOUT IT

- Based on her actions, what do you think Fatima's strengths might be?

- Would you have looked for help if you were in Fatima's situation? Why or why not?

"OK." Fatima grinned. "I have an idea for our next project. Do you mind if I talk about the grades we got on the last one to the group?"

Tanner shook his head. "No. Not if it will help us do better."

When the time came to start their new project, Fatima raised her hand before anyone else could speak.

"If it's OK with everyone else," she said, "I'd like to talk about changing up the group responsibilities."

"What do you mean?" asked Nora, another group member.

"Tanner and I both got lower grades than everyone else on the last project," Fatima explained. "I got lower points because I'm not good at taking notes. Tanner got a lower grade because he doesn't like public speaking."

"Oh no," said Jordan, another member of their group. "I'm sorry. We didn't know!"

"Thanks," Fatima said. "But it's OK. Or I think it can be if we change up the group responsibilities. Tanner could be responsible for the notes, because he's so great at them. I could handle the speaking part of the presentation. Nora, you're so amazing at putting all of our notes together. You could maybe do

the written essay piece? And Jordan, you're super good at artistic stuff. You could put together the presentation poster board?"

Quietly, Tanner chimed in, "That way, we're each showing that we know the material. But in a way that works best for us."

"What do you guys think?" Fatima asked.

Nora and Jordan agreed. The group members started work on the project. Even though they were all working on different

parts of the project, they still worked together to make sure the components fit together.

TALK ABOUT IT

= **How did learning her strengths lead Fatima to success?**

= **How do you think your own strengths could lead to success?**

***

When the day of the presentation came, Fatima was so excited to talk about what she'd learned for more than just a minute or two. She explained her group's chosen theme in-depth, pointing out textual evidence from Tanner's notes and supporting research from Nora's essay, all while using Jordan's poster board as a visual aid. It was fun, and Tanner looked especially relieved that he didn't have to get up and speak.

When the grades came back, Fatima and her group had scored much higher than they ever had before.

"Wow," Fatima enthused. "It worked!"

"And it actually felt easier," Nora agreed. "I always hated doing my piece of the poster board, because putting concepts into pictures doesn't make sense to me. Working mostly on the essay was way less stressful."

"I'm glad." Fatima beamed at her group members. "Hopefully, we can keep doing well by using what we're good at."

ASK THE

EXPERT

Fatima enjoyed English class. But she struggled to be successful in group projects outside of the presentation. Even though Fatima understood the concepts, taking notes and using them to explain those concepts weren't her stronger skills. When Fatima realized this, she analyzed strengths. She realized that she was better at the speaking part of the project, while other people in her group were better at note-taking. After realizing this, Fatima and her group-mates reorganized the project responsibilities to make sure everyone was using their strongest skills. By doing this, Fatima found a way to be successful using what she was good at.

This kind of self-analysis is important. Understanding your strengths can make otherwise challenging situations and assignments seem easier. Instead of scrambling in the face of an obstacle, understanding your strengths gives you a solid way to approach it. Just like Fatima, it can help you turn frustration into success.

But identifying your own strengths can be tricky. Try asking yourself, or others that you trust, what they think you're good at. And once you have a list you agree with, start plotting how you can use those strengths to your best advantage.

GET HEALTHY

- Figure out your strengths. You can do this by asking yourself questions, talking to a teacher or friend, or taking an online strengths quiz.

- Make a list of the ways that your strengths can help you succeed. Think about school, work, and social situations.

- Be a self-advocate. If you know that you'll be more successful trying something that aligns with your strengths, don't be afraid to mention it. Whoever you're talking to may or may not agree, but it's good practice to push for your own well-being.

- Play to the different strengths of group members. That way, you have multiple avenues toward success.

THE LAST WORD FROM KATE

Instead of comparing yourself to those around you, focus on what you can contribute to a situation that no one else can. I've always struggled with hands-on assignments. Anything that required building, assembling, or physically creating was confusing and frustrating for me. But I've always loved words and explaining things on paper. Eventually, I learned that whenever there was a hands-on project, I was better off doing the written portion of the assignment and leaving the physical assembly to those who understood it better.

Part of your identity is understanding what you're good at and figuring out how to apply those skills to things that are more challenging for you. Being able to speak your strengths to the world communicates that identity to others. Even though analyzing your strengths can take time and effort, it's worth it to have your best tools at the ready as you move forward.

CHAPTER THREE

GENDER IDENTITY

U nderstanding your gender identity is an important part of your overall identity. However, while some people don't think about their gender very much, for others, gender can be complicated to figure out. It's not determined by the sex you were assigned at birth, what clothes you like to wear, or whom you are interested in dating. It's also not binary, or something limited to two options. There are more genders than simply male and female. Gender exists on a spectrum of possible genders, which means there is a scale with a range of possible gender identities. Some people are fixed into a certain point on the scale, while other people move back and forth fluidly and may identify as different genders at different times. Some people choose labels that are not on the scale at all, identifying as agender, or genderless.

Any of these options is perfectly OK. You are the best expert of your own self. While clubs and organizations in your school or community can help you understand how to figure out your gender identity, ultimately deciding how to label your gender identity is something that you have to do for yourself.

However, communicating your gender identity, especially if it doesn't match the sex you were assigned at birth, can seem like a scary prospect. Some people don't understand the complexities of gender. It can be tough to correct someone about your gender identity, especially if that person is a trusted adult. That's what happened to Allie in her math class.

> It can be tough to correct someone about your gender identity, especially if that person is a trusted adult.

ALLIE'S STORY

Every day at school, the idea of going to her geometry class made Allie's stomach churn. She loved math, and it had been her favorite subject last year. She'd even won third place in a math competition for her whole school district!

But Allie's problem with her math class wasn't related to the subject matter. Her problem was with her teacher, Mr. James. He'd been Allie's algebra teacher two years ago before he started teaching other math classes. She liked him a lot—he always told

funny jokes to help the class understand new material. However, Mr. James had Allie as a student before she came out as a transgender (trans) girl. A trans person has a gender identity that doesn't match the sex they were assigned at birth.

Allie had changed her name and pronouns since the last time Mr. James was her teacher. And while he was great at teaching how to find the area of a triangle, he wasn't great at remembering Allie's new pronouns. Every time he called Allie by her birth name and not her true name, it made her stomach clench. Every time he referred to Allie with the wrong pronouns, Allie felt like crying. She'd even pretended she had to go to the restroom just so she could leave class for a few moments and take a deep breath.

The few times she or her friends had tried to correct Mr. James, he'd smiled and apologized but forgotten all over again. Allie didn't know what to do. She knew who she was, and so did her friends and family. They'd all accepted her gender identity with love and respect, since Allie knew herself best. Maybe one teacher wasn't worth being upset about. But Mr. James failing to acknowledge Allie's gender identity made Allie feel unseen. It made her feel like she was talking about something important to someone, but the person she was talking

TALK ABOUT IT

- Why do you think Allie was so upset by Mr. James's actions?
- How would you feel if someone ignored part of your identity?

to wasn't even listening. Worst of all, it made her doubt who she knew herself to be.

***

Allie started skipping math class. She couldn't bear the thought of sitting in her desk and being called the wrong name every day, but she wasn't sure how to fix it. Mr. James was a teacher, and Allie didn't want to cause trouble. But eventually, the school caught Allie skipping class, and the assistant principal called her parents. When Allie's parents asked her about it, she explained that Mr. James kept calling her by the wrong name and using the wrong pronouns.

"We're so sorry," said Allie's mom. "That's awful. Skipping class isn't great, but you have every right to be upset at what Mr. James is doing."

Allie's dad asked, "How can we help? What do you need us to do?"

"I'm not sure," Allie said. She picked at a loose thread on her shirt. Talking about this whole thing made her nervous. "Mr. James is my teacher. And I don't think he's calling me the wrong name to be mean. Maybe it's not worth the trouble."

TALK ABOUT IT

= **Do you think Allie's response to the situation was right? Why or why not?**

= **How would you have reacted in Allie's situation? Differently or the same?**

= **How would you handle standing up to an authority figure or adult?**

"It is if you're upset about it," Allie's dad said. "Your identity belongs to you. No one else gets to take it away from you, whether it's one person or a hundred."

"We love you," Allie's mom said. "Whatever you decide to do is your choice. Just know that we're behind you 100 percent of the way."

Allie smiled at both of her parents. "Thanks. I love you guys too. I'm going to sleep on it, OK?"

***

The next day, Allie thought about her dad's words. She thought about how important her identity was to her and how hard she'd fought just to have it. Allie decided to meet with the principal to explain the problem. She asked her parents to come with her.

It was a difficult situation to navigate because Allie didn't want Mr. James to get in trouble. All she wanted was her identity respected with accurate pronouns and her actual name.

TALK ABOUT IT

= **What are your feelings about Allie's parents and how they handled the situation? Would you have done anything differently?**

= **Do you think Allie was right to seek help from her parents? From the principal?**

"I don't think he's trying to upset me on purpose," Allie explained. Her palms were sweaty, and her voice kept shaking, but Allie lifted her chin and powered through it. "But I don't think he understands how important it is to have who you are acknowledged. I just don't know what to do now or how to explain it to him."

"It's not your responsibility to explain it," the principal assured Allie. "The problem needs to be fixed on our end, not yours. Thank you for bringing this to my attention, Allie."

A few days later, the principal brought a person who was an ally for transgender students to the school. He then brought Mr. James to his office, and the three of them had a long conversation behind closed doors.

***

A few days later, Mr. James asked Allie to stay behind after class. "I'm sorry for not respecting your gender identity," he said. "I would never want a student to feel unwelcome in my class."

"Thank you for the apology," Allie said.

"I didn't understand how important it was to you. That's not an excuse—I know I need to do better." Mr. James smiled at Allie. "The transgender ally assigned me some great educational tutorials to complete online about how to better respect different identities and support student needs. They've been a wonderful learning tool. The principal is considering assigning the trainings for the whole school. I hope we can all learn to do better together."

Allie breathed a sigh of relief. "That would actually be really great!"

"I think so. Thank you for reminding me, Allie, that I need to pay more attention to who my students are and not just the work they do."

Allie smiled back. "Wow. You're welcome, I guess."

"I'm going to try harder," Mr. James promised. "Besides," he joked, "I'm supposed to be educating my students—not the other way around, right?"

"Right," Allie said, laughing.

Her stomach was still shaky in the aftermath of all her nerves. But Allie also felt a million times better after sticking to what she knew was true about herself and asking the world to know it too.

TALK ABOUT IT

■ Why did the principal say that speaking to Mr. James wasn't Allie's responsibility? Do you agree?

■ Would you have accepted Mr. James's apology? Why or why not?

ASK THE

EXPERT

Even though Allie was certain of her gender identity, her identity wasn't respected in her math class. Whether or not it was intentional for Mr. James to call Allie by the wrong name and pronouns, it was still a painful experience. Gender dysphoria is distress caused by having a gender identity that doesn't match the sex assigned at birth. A person's dysphoria can become worse if others don't respect their name, pronouns, or other aspects of their gender identity. Allie dreaded the idea of going to class and feeling terrible once she was there.

At first, Allie didn't seek help because she was nervous about the idea of challenging an authority figure. But eventually, with the support of her loved ones, Allie realized that her identity was worth advocating for. She went to the principal, and together they found a solution to the problem.

Gender identity is still a shifting landscape. We're learning more and more about it every day. But change can cause confusion and misunderstanding. That's why it was so important for Allie to stay true to who she knew herself to be. And when her gender identity was being called into question, even indirectly, she looked for help from others to back up her position. Allie knew that she was the best expert of her own self, and she made sure that the people around her knew it as well.

GET **HEALTHY**

- Think about your own gender identity and how you define it. It might be different from what other people expect, or it might be exactly the same. Either one is OK, as long as it's true to who you are.

- Be an ally to others. Instead of looking down on them for being different from you, defend their right to do so by practicing understanding and friendliness.

- Speak up. If you feel like your gender identity is being challenged, you don't have to handle it alone. Tell someone you trust, or contact an organization that can help you advocate.

- Educate yourself on different gender identities. Understanding different terms and options may help you understand where and how you fit on the larger gender spectrum.

THE LAST WORD FROM **KATE**

Sitting down and examining your own gender identity may seem like an intimidating task. It's such a central piece of who you are, and it's easy to get overwhelmed in the process of it. But determining your identity, and especially gender identity, is a personal journey. It's about who you are and who you want to be.

And, however you end up defining your identity, know that you're not alone. Our understanding of gender identity has changed so much in recent years. If you need help, there are far more resources available now to help you figure it out. And once you have figured it out, you can surround yourself with people who support your identity.

CHAPTER FOUR

VALUES

One of the most important parts of growing up is deciding on the values by which you want to live. Values are personal beliefs that act as your inner compass. They help you judge whether things are right or wrong. Values define your identity because they show the world what you find important.

However, deciding on internal values might seem difficult in a world overrun by outside voices. It may feel confusing at first to figure out what you believe in. Often, you inherit values from your parents or other trusted adults in your life, such as religious leaders, teachers, and doctors. Sometimes, your friends and classmates can influence or change your values. As you are figuring out your identity, you might find that your values no longer match the ones you were taught. Or, you might find that you have the same values you grew up with, but your friends and classmates don't feel the same way.

Going against other people to defend your values, especially people close to you, can be intimidating. How do you hold true to your own definition of right and wrong if you feel pressure to change it?

LUPITA'S STORY

Every Thursday night, Lupita and her mother watched their favorite TV show together. They drank hot chocolate and shouted commentary while they watched. Sometimes, they threw popcorn at the screen when their favorite characters made ridiculous decisions. Lupita didn't see her mother very often because she had long work shifts at the hospital, so Lupita looked forward to their time together every week.

However, watching the show with her mom had started to feel different recently. The TV show had added a storyline about one of the main characters dating a Muslim woman. Whenever those characters appeared on screen together, Lupita's mom would frown. Sometimes she would even throw popcorn, as if the two characters were ridiculous— even if they weren't doing

Going against other people to defend your values, especially people close to you, can be intimidating.

anything out of the ordinary! It seemed to be just because one character was Christian and the other was Muslim. Her mom's reaction toward Muslim people made Lupita feel uncomfortable.

Lupita's mother had strongly held beliefs on just about everything. And even when Lupita disagreed with her mom, she didn't voice her opinions. She respected her mom and loved her very much. The idea of fighting with her mom made Lupita feel sick to her stomach and terrified that her mom would never want to watch TV with her again.

TALK ABOUT IT

- Have you ever agreed with something your parents believed just because you didn't want to start a fight?

- Why might Lupita have been so intimidated by the idea of disagreeing with her mother?

49

Lupita's mother thought that people from different religious backgrounds shouldn't get married. She explained, "It's important to support traditional relationships."

But Lupita strongly disagreed. Lupita thought it didn't matter who was in a relationship, as long as everybody involved was happy to be there. She was uncomfortable with her mother's use of the word *traditional*. She felt uneasy about her mother's phrasing and how it suggested that relationships outside of her mother's definition of traditional were somehow wrong or bad. But she kept quiet because she didn't want to argue with her mother.

***

Two weeks later, Lupita's friend Ava invited their entire friend group over to her house after school. After they swam in Ava's pool and ate popsicles on the deck, Ava told her friends that she was now dating a girl named Noor who went to another school in their town. Lupita was shocked to find out that they had been dating for months!

"I waited to tell you all because I wasn't sure how you all would react," Ava said. But she added that she really liked Noor and didn't want to keep her a secret anymore.

Lupita was pleased that her friend group was supportive of Ava's girlfriend. The friends asked a lot of questions. They asked whether they could meet Noor the next time they all hung out together. Ava grinned, obviously relieved at their reaction, and Lupita felt terrible. She felt terrible because she was keeping quieter than the others. Her mother's beliefs about religion and relationships were ringing like a bell inside her head.

At home that night, Lupita felt incredibly torn. She felt caught between the love and loyalty she felt she owed her mother and the strong friendship she felt for Ava. It was so loud inside her head. Her mother's voice was there

TALK ABOUT IT

= What do you think is the source of Lupita's struggle?

= Do you think Lupita really agrees with her mother's values? Why or why not?

51

> Lupita was having trouble finding her own thoughts in the noise of it.

repeating her own beliefs. Ava's voice was there too, explaining how much she enjoyed spending time with Noor. Lupita was having trouble finding her own thoughts in the noise of it. She couldn't tell how she really felt about the situation—only that she disagreed with someone she cared about.

***

A few days later, Ava invited everyone over again. This time, Noor was there too. She made Ava laugh her real laugh, the one that Ava tried to hide sometimes because it made her snort. Lupita liked Noor a lot, and it made the inside of her head feel even louder. She had hoped that meeting Noor would help her make a decision, but if anything, it confused her further.

Lupita went into the kitchen for a snack, and Ava followed her.

"You've been quiet," Ava said. "Ever since I told you guys about dating Noor. Do you have a problem with me dating another girl?"

TALK ABOUT IT

= Why might Lupita feel like she owed Ava an apology? Do you think she did? Why or why not?

= How would you have handled Lupita's situation?

"No, it's not that," Lupita said.

"Is it because Noor is Muslim?" Ava asked.

"My mom would have a problem with that," Lupita said, avoiding the question.

"And you agree with your mom?"

"No," Lupita said. "I like Noor. I can tell that she makes you happy, and to me, that's what matters. But I don't want to fight with my mom."

"You don't have to fight with her," Ava said. "But you're allowed to disagree. Especially about what you think is important."

Something about what Ava said cut through the noise in Lupita's head, quieting it enough that she could make a decision. "You're right," Lupita said. "I'm sorry if I made you feel like your relationship was a problem. I really don't think it is."

"Thank you," Ava replied.

That night, Lupita and her mother watched their favorite TV show together. When the main character defended his girlfriend's

choice about wearing a hijab at work to her boss, Lupita's mother frowned again. She made another comment about supporting traditional relationships.

This time, Lupita was prepared. She said, "I would be more comfortable if you didn't talk about the characters like that anymore."

"Why?" her mom asked.

"I don't think there's anything wrong with a Muslim person and a Christian person dating," Lupita said. "Ava's girlfriend Noor is really sweet, and it hurts my feelings that you'd talk about her like this too."

"Oh," Lupita's mother said. She didn't say anything more on the subject and turned back to the TV. In fact, she didn't make any more comments for the rest of the show. As soon as it was over, Lupita's mother turned off the TV and announced she was going to bed.

Lupita's stomach hurt. She wasn't happy that she and her mother were having a disagreement, but she was proud that she stuck to her convictions and stood up for what she thought was right.

TALK ABOUT IT

= How many of your values do you think come from your family or friends?

= Is there anything you feel strongly about that differs from the people around you? What caused that feeling to develop?

ASK THE

EXPERT

Lupita felt like her mother's beliefs went against her own idea of what was right and important, but she was afraid that voicing her values would cause a fight between her and her mother. But when Lupita realized that listening to her mother's values instead of her own was hurting her friend, Ava, Lupita finally found the words to express her own beliefs.

Values are personal things. That's why they're a part of our own unique identities. This means that you may occasionally find yourself at odds with people who have different ideas of what's important. It's perfectly all right to disagree.

But this can feel especially intimidating if the person you're disagreeing with is older, a friend or family member, or in some kind of position of authority. Sticking to your own beliefs as best you can will help solidify whatever identity you're trying to build.

GET **HEALTHY**

- Find someone you trust and respect, like your parents, teachers, or other family members. Talk to them about what values they think are important. Ask yourself if you agree or disagree.

- Trust your gut. Your own sense of right and wrong is deeply ingrained. You may have an instinctual response to something you think is wrong.

- Don't be afraid to engage in conversation with people about their values. You may agree or disagree, but you could also learn a lot about yourself and what you really believe.

THE LAST WORD FROM **KATE**

It may seem easier to base your values around what your friends, family, or the media think is important. But values are personal beliefs. At the end of the day, only you can decide what you hold important in your life. Sticking to those values, even in difficult situations, can show who you are as a person.

But it's also good to learn how to respect the values of others, so long as those values aren't harming anyone else. We can never really know what someone was raised to think or believe or what experiences shaped their idea of what's important. Respecting the values of others, as well as your own, can also go a long way toward defining your identity. However, you may be confronted with values that are harmful to other people, such as racism, sexism, or other forms of oppression and alienation. In that case, it may feel like you can't respect those values. This is a perfectly acceptable response, and disagreement in that case is understandable.

CHAPTER FIVE

FORMING OPINIONS

Usually, it feels easier when we agree with the people closest to us, even if we secretly disagree with whatever topic is being debated. You might still go along with the popular opinion because it may seem like it promises less confrontation.

However, having your own opinions is an important part of your identity. Your opinions let other people know what you think and believe. As an adult, others will expect that you'll be able to take a stance on something and explain your reasoning. To solidify who you are, you need to be able to form your own conclusions and then speak them well.

But it can be difficult to form your own opinions when there are so many other opinions out there. It can be even more difficult if the opinions you form are opposite those of the people closest to you. You have to form opinions responsibly while using reliable information. This can be challenging in a world saturated with conflicting information. Responsible opinions require research, evidence, and explanation.

So, how do you decide what you believe? And how do you stay firm in those opinions when your friends, family, or classmates disagree? Disagreement can be uncomfortable, but agreement for the sake of pleasing others can lead to conflict.

YUKI'S STORY

The colorful posters promoting the class president campaign papered the hallway. Yuki couldn't walk from class to class without getting blasted by slogans and promises from her fellow classmates. They said things such as, *Vote for Erica and get less homework!* and *Save the Music Program! Vote for Marco today!* Caleb was even promising cheeseburgers for lunch every day if he won the class presidency, but everyone agreed that he probably couldn't make that happen.

The largest posters were pretty, pale blue signs that just said *Vote for Sarah!* Sarah was Yuki's best friend. Yuki had helped them make the signs after Sarah had decided to run for class president. Together they had spilled glitter all over Sarah's bedroom carpet and had spent a frantic 30 minutes vacuuming before Sarah's parents got home.

The day before the election, all Sarah could talk about was the upcoming speech. They were supposed to get up in front of their entire class this afternoon and give a short speech on

why they would be the best fit for class president. "But what if everyone hates it?" Sarah fretted. "What if my hands get all shaky? What if no one votes for me?"

"I don't think that's going to happen," Yuki said.

"You're right," Sarah agreed. "You're my best friend, so I guess I've got one vote no matter what."

That afternoon, Yuki listened as the candidates gave their speeches. Sarah did great. They talked about wanting to extend the study hall period and making sure that students who traveled for sports games could make up their assignments without their

TALK ABOUT IT

= Do you think Sarah was right to assume that Yuki would vote for them? Why or why not?

= Have you ever agreed with a friend because you felt like you owed it to them? Why did you feel that way?

grades suffering. Sarah's hands barely shook at all. But Marco, who went after Sarah, gave an even more compelling speech. He brought up points about the school that Yuki hadn't thought about. He talked about wanting to fix the broken water fountain in the main hallway because the most people passed it on the way to classes. He wanted to hold fundraisers for the music program because it was in trouble. Yuki hadn't even known it was a problem.

Yuki caught herself nodding along with Marco's speech. When the speeches were over, she assured Sarah that they'd done great. But Marco's speech stuck in Yuki's head. Later that night, she researched some of the things Marco had mentioned. Yuki thought about all the times she'd really wanted a drink of water before class but hadn't had time to detour to a working water fountain. She also found out that the school music program was in danger of being reduced because of a lack of funding.

Yuki was torn. Sarah was her best friend, and they really

> Yuki caught herself nodding along with Marco's speech.

TALK ABOUT IT

≡ **How did Yuki practice responsibility in forming her opinions?**

≡ **Why might Yuki's agreement with Marco's speech cause conflict between Yuki and Sarah?**

wanted to be class president. But Yuki agreed with Marco's points. She felt like they were important for the school.

***

The next day, Yuki told Sarah that she planned to vote for Marco. She felt bad about it, but she didn't want to lie to her best friend.

"You're not going to vote for me?" Sarah asked. Their eyes were wide and hurt. "But I thought I was your best friend!"

"You are," Yuki assured her. She felt incredibly guilty about not voting for Sarah but also relieved. It was a strange combination. "And you would be a good class president. But I looked up Marco's points. A lot of what he was saying was important to me."

"I thought what I was saying was important," Sarah said.

"It was," Yuki said. "But I thought Marco's points were more important."

"But extending study hall would give students more time to work. And some teachers don't like when students have to miss important tests or assignments because of away games."

"I know," Yuki said. "But I've almost been late to class myself because of that broken water fountain. And I think cutting down our music program would be bad for the school."

TALK ABOUT IT

= **Do you think Yuki was right to tell Sarah about her vote?**

= **Would you have done the same in Yuki's situation? Why or why not?**

Sarah crossed their arms. "I thought I could at least count on your vote."

"I'm sorry," Yuki said. "But I can't vote for you just because you're my friend. I have to go with what I think is right. Are you mad at me?"

For an agonizingly long minute, Sarah didn't answer. But then they sighed. "No," they said. "You have to go with your own opinion, I guess."

"Thanks," Yuki said. "And I really do think you're great. You might still win!"

Sarah grinned. Yuki grinned back. She was incredibly glad to have a friendship that could make it through disagreements without falling apart.

"I can't vote for you just because you're my friend. I have to go with what I think is right."

TALK ABOUT IT

= Why do you think Yuki and Sarah's friendship was able to survive their disagreement?

= Have you ever disagreed with a friend over an opinion? How did it go?

= Do you think there was a "right" and "wrong" opinion in this situation? Why or why not?

ASK THE
EXPERT

Yuki struggled between supporting her friend and acting on her own opinions. Sarah was excited about being class president and had great ideas. But in Yuki's opinion, Marco's ideas were more important. Even though Yuki didn't want to let her best friend down, she didn't want to let herself down by failing to follow her own values either. In the end, she confessed to Sarah that she thought Marco's points were more important. The friends were able to respectfully disagree, which prevented a possible argument or even the end of their friendship.

What you think and believe is a huge part of who you are. Voicing what you think and believe helps show that identity to the outside world. Sometimes, voicing your opinions can lead to disagreement. It might seem easier to just agree with the opinions of others. But in doing so, your own thoughts and beliefs are minimized. If Yuki hadn't voiced her opinions to Sarah, she would have been giving up what she thought her school needed.

Even though Yuki and Sarah disagreed, they were still able to stay friendly by treating each other's opinions as valid and worthwhile. As long as someone's opinions aren't hurting other people, it's important to disagree respectfully.

GET **HEALTHY**

- When researching an opinion, read information from multiple perspectives. That way, you'll use a more well-rounded pool of information to form your own opinion.

- Don't be afraid to ask questions about opinions—both your own and those of others. Asking questions helps you verbalize what you think more clearly.

- Understand that someone else's opinions may have come from different places or been influenced by other things.

- It can be easy to lose your temper when debating opinions, but do your best to keep the conversation positive. When things turn ugly, people stop listening and considering other points of view.

THE LAST WORD FROM **KATE**

Going against what friends, family, or fellow classmates think can be intimidating. For months, I agreed with a friend's political views because I didn't want to cause problems between us. However, I felt like I was being dishonest about what I really thought and believed. Once I finally voiced what I really thought, I felt better for speaking my mind.

Potentially, one of the hardest things you'll ever have to learn is how to respectfully disagree with the people closest to you. But this skill will come in handy when penning college essays, answering questions in a job interview, or debating issues in class. While sorting through the mass of information needed to figure out exactly where you stand might seem like too much, it can only benefit you to have these things locked down before someone asks you about them.

CHAPTER SIX

GENDER EXPRESSION

How many times have you heard that only boys can like certain things, while only girls can like other things? Maybe you've heard that pink is for girls and blue is for boys, or that girls play with dolls while boys play with trucks and cars. Have you ever been told that girls are better caretakers, while boys are better at math, science, and technology?

These are stereotypes, or beliefs that many people have because they've been repeated over and over until they're thought to be true. And these specific gender stereotypes have to do with what people believe is correct for girls and boys to like or be good at doing.

These stereotypes are especially targeted at young girls and women. Many girls feel enormous pressure to be pretty and datable to boys. They are told not to like movies or toys that boys typically like. You might have seen these stereotypes in TV shows, social media, or in the words and actions of your family.

You might have felt like you are supposed to like something because girls like it, and that not liking it is wrong.

But just as there is more than one gender identity, there are also multiple ways to express gender. Gender expression is how you present yourself and your gender to the world through things such as how you dress, how you act, and what you do. Gender expression isn't just the difference between some things being for boys and other things being for girls. Gender expression can be extremely fluid. This means it can change depending on your mood, the situation you're in, or your personal preference. You may ascribe to more feminine expression, more masculine expression, or a mixture of both.

But going against long-held stereotypes can be challenging. Riley had trouble expressing her gender the way she wanted to because of stereotypes some of her classmates held.

RILEY'S STORY

Riley loved many things. She loved shopping in the boys' section of clothing stores, because she felt the clothes were more comfortable and fit her better. She loved playing for her school's basketball team. She loved watching anime with her boyfriend, Darren, and collecting the figurines from the shows they watched at the conventions they attended. She also hated how tangled her thick hair got when it was long, so she loved wearing it short, sometimes even shaving the back or the side.

Riley was the only one of her group of friends who wore clothes from the boy's section. But it didn't bother her. She was comfortable with who she was and her own way of being a girl. Besides, the people who loved her were great with it too. Darren always cheered her on from the stands during her basketball games. And Riley's friends never failed to invite her when they went to the mall, even though Riley disappeared into different sections of the store. But not everyone was so understanding. One of the boys in Riley's social studies class, Marcus, asked her if she was confused.

"What do you mean?" Riley asked him.

"You just seem like you don't know if you want to be a girl or a boy," Marcus said. "You act like a boy all the time and dress like one too."

Riley was baffled by this. She wasn't confused at all. She knew exactly who she was, and she didn't think that the way she showed it made her less of a girl.

She was comfortable with who she was and her own way of being a girl.

TALK ABOUT IT

- Do you have any hobbies or favorite activities that you think other people might find strange?
- Have you ever experienced people commenting negatively on your clothes or interests? How did it make you feel?

***

In October, Riley was elected to the Homecoming Court. She was thrilled, since she hadn't expected to get nominated by her classmates. Riley and her friends made plans to go shopping for outfits. Riley was excited because she and Darren wanted to wear matching suits and look really stylish together. But Riley's dad frowned at Riley's plan. "Why don't you just let Darren wear the suit, and you can wear a matching dress," her dad said.

"Oh, I hate wearing dresses," Riley said.

"I know," her dad said. "But it's tradition."

Riley didn't want to go against her dad. So, when her friends went shopping for the dance, Riley stuck with them instead of heading for a different section of the store. She tried on dresses with the other girls, but every dress felt stiff and uncomfortable. Riley hated the way they fit her and how she didn't seem like herself when she looked in the mirror.

TALK ABOUT IT

= Do you think that there are such things as "boy things" and "girl things"?

= Have you ever felt like there were things you couldn't do because you were a girl?

"Why waste the money on something you hate?" Darren asked when she called him that night, frustrated after failing to find a dress she even tolerated, let alone liked.

"I don't want my dad to be upset with me," Riley explained. "He said that the girls were expected to wear dresses."

Darren said, "Expected but not required, right? He didn't say that you couldn't go to the dance if you wore a suit, right?"

TALK ABOUT IT

= Have you ever felt pressured to change something about yourself to make other people happy?

= Do you agree with Riley's boyfriend and his idea of tradition? Why or why not?

"He said it was traditional," Riley said.

"Traditional just means that something is old," Darren said. "It doesn't mean that thing is forever. I know it's not my choice. You have to decide what you want to do, and I'll support

whatever it is. But I think you should dress however would make you most comfortable."

"Thanks," Riley said with a smile.

***

On the day of the Homecoming dance, Riley walked down the front steps of her house with Darren. They wore matching suits with red velvet ties. Instead of a corsage and boutonniere, Riley and Darren pinned buttons of their favorite anime characters to each other's lapels. When Riley's dad turned around to take photos of them before the dance, Riley smiled at his noticeable confusion.

"I know you said that girls were expected to wear dresses," Riley explained. "But that's not who I am. Dresses make me uncomfortable. A suit fits me way better."

Riley's dad blinked. "All right. As long as you're comfortable, I guess."

"I am," Riley agreed.

Riley had an amazing time at the dance. She and Darren danced the night away, and she got some great pictures with her friends in the photo booth. But even more than the dance itself, Riley loved that she was able to attend as herself, and not who other people thought she should be.

TALK ABOUT IT

≡ **Would you have made the same choice as Riley?**

≡ **Do you think that there is one right way to be a girl? Why or why not?**

ASK THE

EXPERT

Riley's gender expression was challenged by a school tradition that was based on stereotypical ideas of femininity for girls. Even though Riley was comfortable with who she was and how she expressed herself, she was made to feel like there was something strange or wrong about her identity.

But trying to fit in with that school tradition made Riley unhappy and uncomfortable. It felt dishonest to who she really was. Riley realized, after attempting to fulfill a more stereotypical role, that she couldn't base her happiness in what other people thought a girl should be.

Defining your gender expression can be difficult, especially when there are still stereotypical ideas about the differences between what girls and boys should wear, like, and do. Even with all the progress we've made in understanding that gender is complicated, you could still face pressure to fit in with everyone else if your expression is different from your friends.

But identity, including finding ways to express your gender that make you feel good, is something you build for yourself, not for other people. Basing who you are on what other people think could cause unhappiness.

GET **HEALTHY**

- Challenge the idea that there are defined norms for girls and boys. If someone says a girl can't do something or a boy can't do something, don't be afraid to ask why they think that.

- Try new and different activities, even if you thought they were off limits to you. You never know what you might enjoy.

- Wear what you feel comfortable in. Don't feel pressured to wear clothing that makes you uncomfortable just because it ascribes to certain gender stereotypes.

- Remember that there is no one right way to be a girl. Everyone is unique, interesting, and complex!

THE LAST WORD FROM **KATE**

There are countless ways for a person to be a girl. Expecting someone to express themselves a certain way all because of gender is an old idea. You can be as traditionally masculine or feminine as you want. You can also be a mixture of both. Whatever feels most comfortable and true to who you are is OK. Shaking off stereotypes that have been around for a long while can be difficult. But it can be done as long as everyone stays honest in who they want to be. Overall, how you express yourself is up to you. You're not limited to what others think you should do—only what you want to do.

CHAPTER SEVEN

SOCIAL MEDIA

I f you've ever explored people's profiles on social media, you may have come across what seems like the perfect profile. It may show what looks like a perfect person with incredible fashion sense, adorable pets, fabulous vacations, and a glamorous significant other. It's hard not to get swept up in these accounts and follow someone's interesting, perfect life for inspiration.

We live in a world of ever-increasing social media usage—which isn't necessarily a bad thing. Even though some people grumble about the increasing screen time, social media has some amazing upsides. You're able to stay connected with friends and family members, even outside of school or gatherings. You can connect with people all over the world whom you otherwise might never have had the chance to know. Exploring other people's posted interests can help you discover new interests of your own. And awareness of social issues has increased with our ability to experience them through the eyes of others, such as people using social media as a platform to broadcast protests, debates, and discussions for those not in attendance. This leads to a greater sense of community and support.

However, some dangers are associated with too much social media usage—especially when it comes to forming an identity. Increased social media usage has led to something called impression management, which is when people try to control what others think of them by controlling what others see. Those seemingly perfect social media profiles are examples of someone managing the content that their followers see. They share only the best parts of their lives and themselves. It may seem like they never experience hardship or failure because they only post the positive. Looking at these idealized profiles might encourage you to compare yourself to them, even if what you see isn't really the truth.

Comparing yourself to others can hinder your own self-discovery. You may feel the need to create an almost separate, seemingly perfect self on your social media profiles. You may post things that aren't the truest representation of you and your life just to keep up with the profiles around you. The pressure of maintaining this semi-fictionalized identity can be exhausting. Connie learned that while trying to create an Instagram profile that looked more like her friends' accounts.

CONNIE'S STORY

Connie created her Instagram account because she wanted
to have a place to showcase her love for baking. Trying out
new recipes helped her unwind after a long day of school and
extracurricular activities such as the graphic design club.
Her account became a fun way to document different baking
challenges that she set for herself—unique cookie recipes,
brownies that went above and beyond regular chocolate
concoctions, and towering cakes with complicated icing that
let her incorporate her passion for graphic design. Soon, people
from all over the world followed her account and complimented

her final products. They also offered recipes to try and gave her tips to improve her baking skills.

Connie followed her friends' Instagram accounts too. At first, it was a great way to stay in touch outside of school. They supported each other's pictures and posts. It made Connie feel like they were even closer because they could share more of themselves than they could during a typical school day.

But then at school, her friends started talking about all the attention they'd received on certain posts.

"I've gained 17 new followers in the last day!" Connie said before updating her story.

"I just hit 2,000!" Caleb said, prompting Min-jun to give him a high-five.

Connie's friend Basil even said that people were reaching out about the artwork zie had posted. Followers were asking whether Basil would create drawings for them.

Connie hadn't paid much attention to her number of followers. But now she noticed that it was smaller than

"I've gained 17 new followers in the last day!"

Basil's and her other friends'. She wondered why. She thought it might be because she was only posting recipes and photos of her baking successes and failures. Basil posted hir artwork and pictures of hir pets. Min-jun posted videos of his dance rehearsals and beautiful photos of all the places he traveled for his dance competitions. And Caleb's dashboard was filled with pictures of him and his basketball teammates having all sorts of fun and silly adventures around town.

Connie started posting new types of photos on Instagram in order to gain more followers. She posted pictures of her super cute golden retriever, Missy. After graphic design club, she'd post about what she'd been working on. Connie didn't have fancy travel pictures, but she started looking for pretty places around her own hometown to document. And whenever she went somewhere with her friends, even if they were just biking to the gas station, she made sure to detail it on her Instagram story.

In the wake of increased posting, Connie's follower count went up. However, her friends' follower counts were increasing too. Their photos looked perfect. On Tuesday, Caleb posted a photo of the park down the street, which Connie had posted a few days earlier. But Caleb's

TALK ABOUT IT

▪ **Why do you think Connie felt pressure to change her social media profile?**

▪ **Have you ever posted something on social media because you wanted more followers? Why or why not?**

83

photo was much more interesting than hers. He'd managed to get a video of one of his teammates making a basket from the half-court line.

Connie felt like she couldn't keep up or make her photos as interesting as those of her friends or the other accounts that she followed on her dashboard. Posting a new picture or funny little story every day became a necessity, even when Connie's heart wasn't in it. But instead of looking at new recipes or ways to improve her baking, Connie carefully tracked the amount of attention each post earned. When a post didn't earn as much attention as the one before it, Connie felt like she'd done something wrong. Every lost follower filled her with a sense of dread.

Her friends made increasing their follower count seem so effortless. They always had incredible things to post.

Connie started to resent every picture or story they posted because it reminded her that she had nothing to compare.

***

One day, Basil burst into tears in the middle of lunch. Basil said that zie was so exhausted from trying to meet everyone's commission requests for personalized artwork. Even opening the Instagram app made hir anxious, because zie knew there would be more requests waiting.

TALK ABOUT IT

= Do you think social media has an effect on self-esteem? If so, do you think it's positive, negative, or both?

= Have you ever felt like you were pretending to be someone you're not in your social media posts?

"Really?" Connie asked. "You keep posting how #blessed you are that people want your drawings so badly."

"And your posts of the finished drawings always get thousands of likes," Min-jun added. "People love what you're posting."

"That's because I only post what people want to see!" Basil said, rubbing hir hands over hir face. "Everyone wants me to be this amazing art account. I can't just stop and say, 'actually, I'd love to talk about sports, or what I'm up to in school.'"

"It's stressing you out?" Caleb asked.

Basil nodded. "I'm constantly working on art. Every minute that I'm not in school, I'm drawing or inking or editing my photos," zie said. "Last night I was awake until two o'clock in the morning trying to get some posts ready for today. I'm starting to not like drawing anymore."

"Yikes," Min-jun said. "Why don't you just stop?"

"Because it's my thing now," Basil said. "I've got all these followers, and they want me to post new art every day. They don't want drawings once a week and photos of my coffee or my stack of textbooks the other days of the week. If I started to post like that, there's a million other amazing artists they could follow instead."

Connie felt terrible for Basil and how stressed zie seemed. But Basil's situation also made Connie think about her own social media profile. Just like Basil, Connie wasn't even having fun with it anymore. All she did was try and find bigger and more interesting things to post so that people would think she was a super-cool person like her friends.

That night, Connie tried to avoid Instagram. She even put her phone in her sock drawer to keep herself from posting anything new. She didn't update her account the next day either. Almost an entire week went by before she made a new Instagram post, and that was only

because she found a fun new recipe for macarons that she wanted to try.

Connie lost some of her followers, but she was happier with how she used her Instagram profile. She only posted photos when she wanted to, and she didn't feel the need to document every single thing she did. She even encouraged Basil to take a break from posting artwork, which meant zie had time to come over after school and help Connie whip up a Black Forest cake.

Connie didn't delete her Instagram account or her other social media profiles because she still thought it was a great way to connect with people. But she didn't want to spend all of her time trying to make herself into someone that she wasn't.

ASK THE
EXPERT

At first, Connie's social media profile was a fun way to keep track of a hobby she enjoyed. However, trouble came when Connie started comparing her social media profile to her friends' profiles. She felt pressure to get as many followers as her friends, so she posted more frequently in order to keep up with her rising follower count. By the end of it, something Connie had enjoyed at first became a chore that was causing stress and anxiety. She no longer enjoyed posting to Instagram, and the things she did post were no longer true to her identity.

It can be incredibly easy to fall into this kind of comparison game. You're trying to live up to another person's best moments without stopping to consider that maybe they're only posting the good and hiding the bad. Connie spent so much time comparing her profile to her friend Basil's. But Connie and her other friends were completely shocked when Basil revealed that hir social media was causing hir daily distress. After this, Connie made the decision to only post on her social media when she really felt like it and when she had something she was genuinely excited to share.

Social media can be a wonderful, amazing tool that can help people figure out their identities. But make sure that the identity you're creating is true to you.

GET **HEALTHY**

- ⹅ Approach the social media profiles of others with a healthy dose of reality. Remember that everyone has struggles in their life, even if they're not posting about them online.

- ⹅ Talk to your friends to determine how they're doing. Chances are there's more going on than the pictures and posts they allow on their profiles.

- ⹅ Try to post things you feel excited about sharing. Getting followers is not a competition. Remember that social media exists to help you share what you love!

- ⹅ If you're feeling overwhelmed, don't be afraid to turn off the social media for a while. You don't have to get rid of it. But sometimes a little separation can help clear your head.

THE LAST WORD FROM **KATE**

Figuring out who you are in a social media society can be tough. While you are figuring out your identity, you also have to decide how you want people to perceive it. Moderating what people think about you by controlling what they see might seem like a great thing. But you risk creating a false identity, which can then be stressful to maintain.

So how do we avoid this constant desire to compete with others online? It comes down to sticking with what you're truly excited about and interested in, and letting that guide what you post. Lean on the many amazing benefits of social media, such as sharing and connecting with people all over the world. Instead of comparing yourself to others, focus on creating a profile that is a true representation of who you want to be.

CHAPTER EIGHT

CHECKING MORE THAN ONE BOX

Has anyone ever asked you, "Where are you from?" and then followed up by asking, "No, where are you *really* from?" People often use these questions to find out someone's race or ethnic roots, but they may not realize how offensive the questions can be. Typically, someone receives this question when they do not share the same racial identity as the majority of people in their community. While the asker may think that it's an innocent question, often the implication is that they think someone doesn't belong.

But what does it mean to belong to a certain race or ethnic group? Before 2010, the US Census only allowed people to check one box in the race category. This meant that even if people had one parent from one race and another parent from another race, they would have to choose one identity. However, starting with the 2010 census, people could check as many boxes as they wanted to fit their racial identity.

You may be struggling with your own racial identity, or you may have friends who are struggling with theirs. Some teens may feel like they aren't enough of one race to fit in with others in that group, or they may feel like they are *too much* of something else. Some people may have a multiracial background but choose to identify as one race. Others may think about their racial identity differently at school, at home, and at work. This is the case with Gabby, who felt differently about her race when she was at her mostly-white private school versus when she played at home with friends from her neighborhood who looked more like her.

> Some teens may feel like they aren't enough of one race to fit in with others in that group.

GABBY'S STORY

"Good game, Gabby!" shouted Lily, Gabby's friend on the basketball team. They'd both made the junior varsity team as

freshmen, so they'd bonded immediately over a desire to improve their skills and show they deserved their spots on the team.

Lily clapped Gabby on the shoulder. "That last-minute steal was amazing! You could hardly tell it's been something that you've worked on in practice."

"Thanks!" Gabby responded. "I still need to work on my free throws, though. I don't understand how you can sink those so easily. Do you still want to grab food after this?"

"Definitely," Lily said. "I've got to tell you about what happened in class today."

Gabby laughed. Lily always had a new story about the boy in her class who she had a crush on. "OK, I'll see you in the locker room. I'm going to talk to my parents."

"See you later!"

Gabby easily spotted her family among other parents and friends. Most of the students at Gabby's private school were white, so her father and brother's brown skin stood out in the crowd. Gabby's mom was white, but while she may have looked like many of the other parents, she was easy to find because of her loud laughter that echoed throughout the gym.

As Gabby walked toward her family, she was stopped along the way by the parents of several of her teammates. They all congratulated Gabby on the good game and noted how well she played. Gabby hadn't thought this game was particularly special—sure, she had that steal in the last quarter, but she'd also missed several close baskets. Gabby waved and started walking toward them. On her way, some parents of other girls on the team complimented her.

"Great job, Gabby!" one teammate's dad said. "You were born to play!"

"You really have a natural talent," another teammate's mom told her.

Gabby nodded and thanked people who spoke to her, but the interactions also left a sour taste in her mouth. She felt

TALK ABOUT IT

= What are some stereotypes that Gabby faces in school? How might these be different in other places?

= Why do you think Gabby is upset even though people are complimenting her?

= Why do you think Gabby got along best with Lily?

singled out by the attention, which seemed to focus on her natural talent at the sport, as if she hadn't spent all last week practicing her moves! Sometimes, Gabby felt frustrated as the only black player on the team. Instead of commenting on her hard work or dedication to the team, everyone always pointed out that she was born to play basketball. Gabby felt like they made those comments because she was black.

Soon, Gabby reached her family through the crowd.

"Gabby! Way to go!" Her father gave her a hug.

"**Let me celebrate my win for a minute!**"

"Yeah, lucky shot at the end," her brother said. "Your form wasn't quite right, but you got the ball in."

"Let me celebrate my win for a minute!" Gabby laughed. Her brother, who played on the varsity boys' team, was *so* competitive! "You can correct me all you want when we play tomorrow."

***

The next day, Gabby and her brother played basketball with some neighborhood friends. They played basketball together on Saturdays. Gabby loved seeing her friends, especially since she and her brother went to a school outside the neighborhood, while everyone else went to the high school down the street.

Gabby stole the ball from a boy on the other team and whooped as she ran down the court. People on both teams laughed too. "Ben, that was just like when Shauna dunked on you in math class yesterday," one boy said as Gabby went for a lay-up.

"No kidding," Ben said. "That was *brutal*. She even got the teacher laughing!"

"What happened yesterday?" Gabby asked, handing the ball off as she jogged to half-court. "Did someone finally tell Ben that his jokes aren't funny?"

"Ha ha," Ben said sarcastically. "It was—"

"No time for chatting!" Gabby's brother said. "They're still beating us by ten points, and I don't want to buy the celebratory sodas after the game."

Gabby frowned, but she got in position to defend. Ever since they'd started at their new school, Gabby had sometimes felt left out among her neighborhood friends. She was out of the loop on not just gossip, but other more important things going on in her friends' lives. Additionally, Gabby liked her school, but she often felt out of place there as one of the only black students.

After the game, which her team ended up losing, Gabby and her brother waited in line at the convenience store to buy sodas for the winning team. "What's up with you?" her brother asked as they set the items on the counter. "You seemed really down in the second half. I know you're not tired, 'cause you practically ran all the way here."

Gabby frowned. "I felt weird. Do you ever feel like we don't belong anywhere? Like, not at school, not at home?"

Her brother paid for the sodas, then handed Gabby one of the plastic bags as they walked out of the store.

"Do you ever feel like we don't belong anywhere? Like, not at school, not at home?"

"Sometimes," he said. "It can be hard when people at school don't understand where I'm coming from. But I just think about how *I* know who I am, and that makes it a bit easier."

Gabby frowned even deeper. "But what if I don't know who I am yet?"

Her brother smiled. "That's OK, sis," he said. "You have time to figure it out. Plus," he added, clapping her on the shoulder just like Lily had done at the game the night before, "you'll always belong with me. Unless you keep losing basketball games."

Gabby laughed. "Hey!" she shouted, bumping her brother with her shoulder. But he really had made her feel better. Gabby didn't have all the answers yet for how she felt about her identity, but she knew she had people to talk to about it. Just like her brother said, she had plenty of time.

TALK ABOUT IT

= What do you think are benefits and challenges of being in the spotlight?

= Gabby has different experiences at home and school. Can you relate to her? What could be difficult about feeling or acting different depending on who is around you?

98

ASK THE

EXPERT

Playing in different settings mimicked how Gabby felt about being from a mixed-race family. She felt out of place at her school for being one of the only black kids, but she also felt out of place in her neighborhood because she could no longer relate as strongly with her black friends. This led her to feel like she didn't belong anywhere, when that wasn't the case at all.

Social pressures can make girls feel like they have to choose between multiple parts of their identity. Teachers, coworkers, or friends may believe stereotypes about your family origin, financial status, physical abilities, or intelligence because of your race or ethnicity. Even if people don't mean to be offensive, it can still be challenging to educate these people or answer inappropriate questions. Finding a supportive community is important. While Gabby found support with her brother, who had many shared experiences, a supportive community can go beyond people in your family.

Your feelings and life experiences are unique. Your identity belongs to you alone. You don't have to answer questions of origin or try to fit in one box even though some social pressures might try to define you.

GET **HEALTHY**

- Visit places in your community that celebrate diversity.

- Avoid asking questions of origin based on appearance.

- Get to know someone over time or be specific about a question to show respect for someone's personal information.

- Take time to explore your own racial identity. Your feelings, family, traditions, physical features, and life experiences are all part of your unique identity.

THE LAST WORD FROM **KATE**

It can be hard to feel like you belong to a group, especially if there are differences between you and everyone else. Some people have a hard time accepting those who are different. But I've found that each and every person has a community where they belong. It may just take some digging to find those people. Some of my best friends are people I've met in online support groups who live all over the United States! Racial identity may be a hard part of your identity to figure out, or it may be incredibly simple. However, it's OK to take as much time as you need to figure out *any* part of your identity, no matter how large or how small.

A SECOND
LOOK

It might be helpful to think of identity as a patchwork quilt, which is a type of blanket. It's made of different squares of fabric that are sewn together. Each piece plays an important part in creating the bigger, beautiful final design. Your identity is the same. Your experiences and ideals are the smaller pieces that you stitch together to create the final design of who you are.

I mentioned finding my own identity in chicken nuggets, science class, and superhero debates with fellow students. Your identity may come from different places or experiences. The girls in these stories faced issues with school, family, and friends. They collected pieces of themselves by understanding their gender identity and expression, values, internal thoughts, external influences, and struggles. The situations weren't always comfortable. Some pieces of their identities were easier to find than others. But each situation had the benefit of teaching the girl in question to understand herself. Once she was able to do this, she could better communicate who she was to the world around her.

Finding the pieces of your identity can seem overwhelming. The idea of experiences shaping who you are might feel scary. But you'd be amazed at how much of your identity is solidified by your daily decisions—even the ones you don't think about! You'll continue growing and changing throughout your entire life. Your identity will grow and change as well. This means that there's no one right answer to the question of who you are. Who you are may be different than who you were before or even who you want to be in the future. The decision of your identity is always in your hands. That means you, and only you, have the final say in who you are and where you stand in the world.

YOUR FRIEND,
KATE

PAY IT
FORWARD

Figuring out your identity is a long process. It doesn't just happen overnight. Now that you know what to focus on, you can pay it forward to a friend too. Remember the Get Healthy tips throughout this book, then take these steps to get healthy and get going.

1. Be a friend and lend a helping hand to others. We're all going through the process of figuring out who we are. A solid wall of support and unity between girls can make it easier!

2. Spend time educating yourself on the different aspects of gender. This can help you figure out where you fit on the spectrum and also be a better friend and ally to others.

3. Don't buy into gender stereotypes. Explore different activities, interests, mannerisms, and clothing choices. You are not defined by someone else's idea of what a girl should be!

4. When deciding on your values, focus on what's important to you, not other people. Make lists. Ponder your beliefs. Learn to speak them with pride.

5. Develop interests that are uniquely yours. Having different interests from your friends is healthy.

6. When forming opinions, put in the work behind them. Do research and seek out information that agrees with and opposes what you think. That way, your opinions are well-rounded and informed.

7. How you disagree with people says a lot about who you are. Strive to be respectful. Seek honest conversation instead of angry argument.

8. Take time to figure out what you're good at and how you can use those strengths to help yourself succeed.

9. Practice a healthy attitude toward social media. Enjoy its amazing benefits, but don't compare yourself to others. Your story, journey, and identity are your own and won't look the same as anyone else's!

10. When facing hardship or struggles, keep a healthy mindset. Use your struggle as a springboard for growth instead of a reason to despair.

GLOSSARY

advocate
To speak up for yourself.

align
To line up with something, either literally or metaphorically.

ally
A person or group who gives help to another person or group.

boutonniere
A flower pinned to the lapel of a suit jacket for a formal event such as a wedding or dance.

corsage
A bouquet of flowers worn around someone's wrist for a formal event such as a wedding or dance.

fluid
Changeable rather than fixed.

gender expression
The outward appearance of someone's gender identity.

gender identity
A person's perception of their gender, which may or may not correspond with the sex they were assigned at birth.

hijab
A hair and neck covering that is worn by some Muslim women as part of their faith.

ingrained
Established; difficult to change.

reliable
Trustworthy.

stereotype
A widely held but oversimplified idea about a particular type of person or thing.

ADDITIONAL
RESOURCES

SELECTED BIBLIOGRAPHY

Khoo, Isabelle. "4 Reasons Asking 'Where Are You From?' Is Offensive." *HuffPost Canada*, 24 Aug. 2016, huffingtonpost.ca. Accessed 10 Dec. 2019.

Killermann, Sam. "The Genderbread Person." *It's Pronounced Metrosexual*, 2017, genderbread.org. Accessed 2 Oct. 2019.

Office of Adolescent Health. "Healthy Friendships in Adolescence." *U.S. Department of Health and Human Services*, 25 Mar. 2019, hhs.gov. Accessed 2 Oct. 2019.

FURTHER READINGS

Harris, Duchess, and Nancy Redd. *Growing Up a Girl*. Abdo, 2018.

Kay, Katty, and Claire Shipman. *The Confidence Code for Girls*. HarperCollins, 2018.

ONLINE RESOURCES

Booklinks
NONFICTION NETWORK
FREE! ONLINE NONFICTION RESOURCES

To learn more about finding your identity, please visit **abdobooklinks.com** or scan this QR code. These links are routinely monitored and updated to provide the most current information available.

For more information on this subject, contact or visit the following organizations:

Girls Inc.

120 Wall Street
New York, NY 10005
girlsinc.org

Girls Inc. empowers and educates girls to break through barriers. The site includes news, opinion pieces, and chapters for girls to join around the country.

Girls Leadership

111 Myrtle Street, Suite 101
Oakland, CA 94607
girlsleadership.org

Girls Leadership is a nonprofit organization that works with girls and their caregivers, parents, and teachers to instill values of leadership, responsibility, and advocating for one's values.

National Center for Transgender Equality

1133 Nineteenth St. NW, Suite 302
Washington, DC 20036
transequality.org

The National Center for Transgender Equality (NCTE) is dedicated to achieving social justice and equality for transgender people.

INDEX

ABOUT THE
AUTHOR

KATE MORROW

Kate Morrow is a writer and former teacher. She loves reading, writing, and failing at video games.